Piano
Vocal
Guitar

BEST OF
JOHN
PIZZARELLI

20 GREAT SONGS FEATURING THE SONGWRITING TEAM OF
JOHN PIZZARELLI & JESSICA MOLASKEY

ADAM AND EVE	3
DA VINCI'S EYES	9
DAY I FOUND YOU	15
DRY MARTINI	21
THE GIRL WITH HIS SMILE AND MY EYES	27
THE GREEDY TADPOLE	34
HOW COME YOU AIN'T GOT ME	45
I TRIED TOO HARD FOR TOO LONG	50
I WOKE UP EARLY ONE MORNING	54
I WOULDN'T TRADE YOU	60
KISSES IN THE RAIN	64
KNOWING YOU	68
LIFETIME OR TWO	73
OH HOW MY HEART BEATS FOR YOU	78
A RARE DELIGHT OF YOU	82
THE RIVER IS BLUE	87
SAIL AWAY	93
SOMEONE TO COOK FOR	97
SOMETHING LIKE LOVE	104
TAKE A LOT OF PICTURES (IT LOOKS LIKE RAIN)	109

ISBN 978-1-4234-6908-7

HAL•LEONARD®
CORPORATION

7777 W. BLUEMOUND RD. P.O. BOX 13819 MILWAUKEE, WI 53213

Visit Hal Leonard Online at
www.halleonard.com

PREFACE

When I formed my trio in 1990, I was always on the hunt for songs like the Nat Cole Trio had: good "rhythm" songs. It was really how it came to be that I started writing for the trio. If I couldn't find what I wanted, I wrote it. That is how the songs "Oh How My Heart Beats for You" and "Day I Found You" came to pass.

It was also around this time, 1996 to be exact, that I met Jessica Molaskey while doing a Broadway show with her. I was showing her some of my tunes and she would give her feedback, and then point out things to improve them. I was very hard-headed about it at first, but when she would leave, I would make all of her changes ("Lifetime or Two" is just one example). Her instincts were always right. We got married soon afterward and got a real head of steam behind our writing. It was something we really enjoyed doing.

The process was not just one of "my melody / her lyric," though. It worked in a lot of different ways: Jess would have a lyric and a melody and I would harmonize it ("I Woke Up One Early Morning"), or I would have a melody and no lyric ("A Rare Delight of You"). We would be commissioned to write a piece about one of the Seven Deadly Sins ("The Greedy Tadpole"), or I would give Jess a title and she would finish the song ("Dry Martini," "Take a Lot of Pictures").

These are just a few examples. We have written everywhere, too: on planes, trains, backyards, lakefronts and in our New York City apartment. It is a fun and satisfying process no matter how we get to the end, and we are happy to share a number of our songs here with you.

Enjoy!
John Pizzarelli
2012

ADAM AND EVE

By JOHN PIZZARELLI
and JESSICA MOLASKEY

Medium Swing

(Boom doo da doo da doo n da n da da da da n doo da doo da doo da

doot uh.) Ad - am and Eve, they real - ly blew it with that

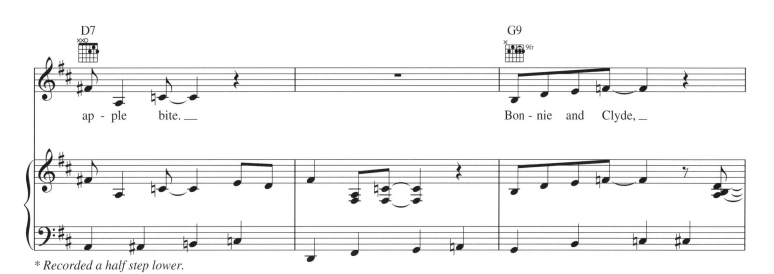

ap - ple bite. Bon - nie and Clyde,

* Recorded a half step lower.

DA VINCI'S EYES

By JOHN PIZZARELLI
and JESSICA MOLASKEY

DAY I FOUND YOU

By JOHN PIZZARELLI

DRY MARTINI

By JOHN PIZZARELLI
and JESSICA MOLASKEY

THE GIRL WITH HIS SMILE AND MY EYES

By JOHN PIZZARELLI
and JESSICA MOLASKEY

Lyrics:
Cross - ing the bridge ___ on the way ___ ___ to the air - port, leav - ing ___ the

THE GREEDY TADPOLE

By JOHN PIZZARELLI
and JESSICA MOLASKEY

Moderate Swing

Once there was a tad-pole who said,"I'm fond ___ of a nice ___

___ piece of land ___ just be - yond ___ my pond," ___ and he

want - ed and want - ed that place for his own, ___ so he

*Lead vocal written an octave higher than sung.

HOW COME YOU AIN'T GOT ME

By JOHN PIZZARELLI
and JESSICA MOLASKEY

1. You got a smile that hides a
2. You buy one tick-et, and you

3. Instrumental solo

thou-sand punch-lines. ___ You got a nose that Cyr-
win the Lot-to. ___ You set the tone for what

a - no would die ___ for. ___ You got to Pat-sy's and you
the swells are wear-ing. ___ You down mar-ti-nis; oth-er

* Recorded a half step higher.

I TRIED TOO HARD FOR TOO LONG

By JOHN PIZZARELLI
and JESSICA MOLASKEY

I WOKE UP EARLY ONE MORNING

By JOHN PIZZARELLI
and JESSICA MOLASKEY

I WOULDN'T TRADE YOU

By JOHN PIZZARELLI
and JESSICA MOLASKEY

KISSES IN THE RAIN

By JOHN PIZZARELLI

KNOWING YOU

By JOHN PIZZARELLI
and JESSICA MOLASKEY

LIFETIME OR TWO

By JOHN PIZZARELLI
and JESSICA MOLASKEY

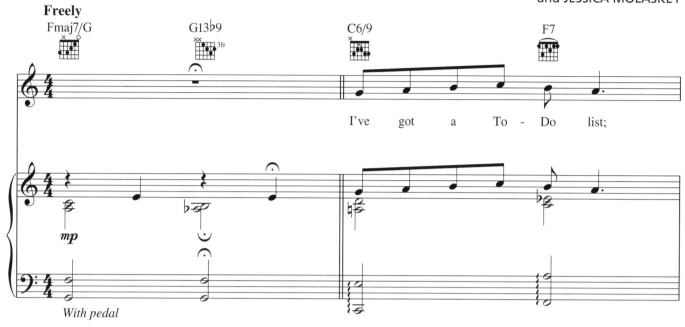

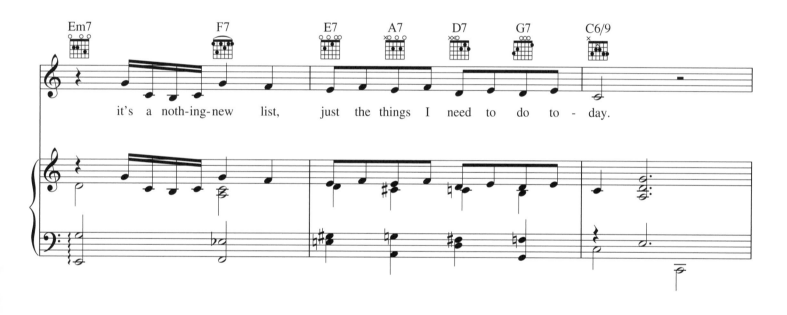

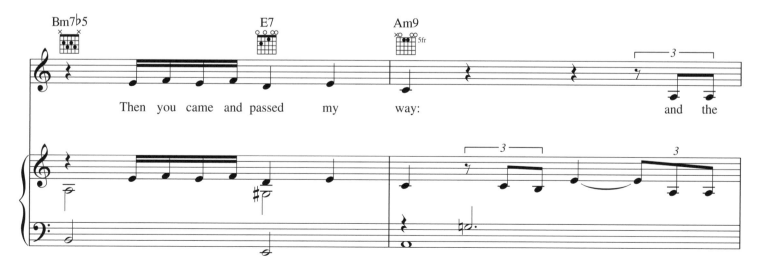

OH HOW MY HEART BEATS FOR YOU

By JOHN PIZZARELLI

CODA

Oh, how my heart beats ___ for

you. _____

A RARE DELIGHT OF YOU

By JOHN PIZZARELLI
and JESSICA MOLASKEY

Something's dif-f'rent _____ in the air _____ to-night, the rare _____ de-light of you. _____ Sure-ly

RIVER IS BLUE

By JOHN PIZZARELLI

* Pronounced "treestay", Brazilian for sadness.

SAIL AWAY

By JOHN PIZZARELLI
and JESSICA MOLASKEY

SOMEONE TO COOK FOR

By JOHN PIZZARELLI
and JESSICA MOLASKEY

SOMETHING LIKE LOVE

By JOHN PIZZARELLI
and JESSICA MOLASKEY

TAKE A LOT OF PICTURES
(It Looks Like Rain)

By JOHN PIZZARELLI
and JESSICA MOLASKEY